Best-Ever Activities for Grades 2-3

Time & Money

**Dozens of Activities With Engaging Reproducibles That
Kids Will Love . . . From Creative Teachers Across the Country**

BY DEBORAH ROVIN-MURPHY AND FRANK MURPHY

D1716186

SCHOLASTIC
PROFESSIONAL BOOKS

New York • Toronto • London • Auckland • Sydney • Mexico City
New Delhi • Hong Kong • Buenos Aires

For my mom, Pat Rovin, who always makes time for me.
—D.R.M.

For my dad, who has given me
so much time and so so much money!!!
—F.M.

Our thanks to all the teachers who contributed ideas to this book:
Peg Arcadi, Stacey Brandes, Jackie Clarke, Eileen Delfini, Mitzi Fehl,
Barbara Gauker, Bob Krech, Sue Lorey, Becky Mandia, Judy Meagher,
Bobbie Williams, and Wendy Wise-Borg.

Produced by **Joan Novelli**
Cover and interior design by **Holly Grundon**
Cover and interior art by **Paige Billin-Frye**

ISBN 0-439-29648-x

CONTENTS

CONTENTS

About This Book

Second and third graders are always ready and eager to learn about their world. In particular, the things that adults do and use often fascinate them. This includes time and money. Second and third graders want to know about time. They love to wear watches, keep track of what's happening when, and show that they can tell time! Even if they haven't yet learned to tell time, it's always on their mind: What time's gym? When's recess? How long until lunch? Money is just as much on their minds. Children delight in opportunities to explore money in real-life situations, using real or play money to learn more about the way it works in the world.

Time falls under the National Council of Teachers of Mathematics (NCTM) standard that addresses measurement. The standard states that "the curriculum should include measurement so that students can understand the attributes of time" and that students need to be able to "make and use estimates of measurement" and "make and use measurements in problems and everyday situations." Money falls under the NCTM standard that covers numbers and operations. The standards state that students should use multiple models to develop understanding of the place-value structure of the base-ten number system and be able to represent and compare whole numbers and decimals. Certainly, money is one of the models that students will enjoy using.

This book is full of engaging activities that support the standards and will enrich your classroom explorations of time and money. Though the activities are organized by the topics of time and then money, you'll find that many of them make interdisciplinary connections. For example, Tissue-Box Time Lines invites children to write about their days as they explore the passage of time in their lives. (See page 14.) Time Around the World makes a geography connection, as children play a time zone game. (See page 11.) Poetry Money Math combines language arts and math with "Smart," a humorous poem by Shel Silverstein. (See page 27.) Other things you'll find in these pages include:

- ideas from teachers across the country

- support for the many ways your students learn, including activities that link math with writing, art, music, and movement

- activities that correlate with the NCTM standards

- hands-on science connections

- strategies for second-language learners

- skill-building morning-message ideas

- literature-based language arts activities

- interactive displays that encourage children to collaborate in their learning

- test-taking and assessment tips

- computer connections, including software and Web site suggestions

- graphic organizers

- ready-to-use take-home activities

- and many more ideas that will have your students making time and money connections to the real world.

Eat the Clock!

Introduce students to the parts of the clock with this delicious hands-on activity.

Y ou'll need flour tortillas or large round crackers (one per student), carrot or celery sticks (two per child), raisins, mini-chocolate chips, and paper towels or paper plates.

⑥ Arrange the clock-making materials on a table and have children help themselves to the "parts." (Or prepackage the materials in sandwich bags and give one to each child.)

⑥ Ask children to look at the classroom clock. Guide them to notice the clock face, the minute and hour hands, the numbers (count by fives), and the marks between the numbers. Let children guess which food they could use to represent each part.

⑥ Model for children how to make a clock, using the tortilla for the clock face, the raisins for the 5-minute intervals, the chocolate chips for the minute intervals, and the carrot or celery sticks for the minute and hour hands. As you place the raisins and chips on the clock, show students how to start at the top, placing a raisin in the 12 spot, then placing four chips to represent the minutes between the 12 and 1. Follow with a raisin, and ask students what it represents. (*the 1 on the clock face*) Continue, counting minutes as you arrange the materials to create the hours and minutes all the way around.

⑥ Let children make their own clocks, then invite them to "eat the clock!" Call out different times, starting with the correct time—for example, 12:15. Have students move the hands to show the time, then eat the parts of the clock that represent that time. Continue, letting them make different times and eat their way around the clock!

Eileen Delfini
Richboro Elementary
Richboro, Pennsylvania

Check for food allergies before children eat their clocks.

SECOND
Language
LEARNERS

H elp multilingual students make the connection between time-telling words in English and in their own language. Use a different-colored marker to write these words and phrases in students' native languages. Display these next to the English time-telling words and phrases.

It's About Time Word Wall

Kick off your unit on time by brainstorming key vocabulary associated with time.

Ask students to share any words they know that are connected to time (and don't forget the calendar!)—for example, *time, clocks, minutes, hours, seconds, half past, quarter after, o'clock, a.m., p.m., nighttime, daytime, alarm*. Record the words on posterboard precut in alarm clock shapes and display at children's eye level. Keep blank word cards handy so that students can add to the word wall as they learn more.

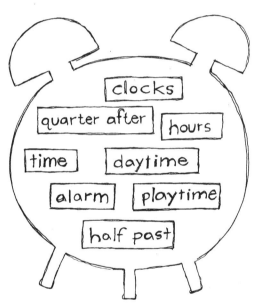

Me Counting Time: From Seconds to Centuries

by Joan Sweeney (Dragonfly, 2001)

This easy-to-read, colorful picture book is perfect for introducing the study of time. It answers the questions: How long is a second? Can you count a minute? What is a decade? How many years are in a century?

Why do we have 60 seconds in a minute and 60 minutes in an hour? The ancient Babylonians divided each hour in a day into 60 equal parts. Later, the Romans used the same system and called each part *par minuta* (a minute). The Romans also divided the minute into 60 equal parts called *par seconda* (a second).

The Fives Have It

Getting students to recognize that the numbers on the clock (1–12) represent groups of five can be difficult at first. Help students make the connection between the numbers on the clock and groups of five with the following activities.

⊚ Post index cards next to the numbers telling the minutes on the classroom clock—for example, next to the 1 have the number 5, next to the 2 have the number 10, next to the 3 have the number 15. When practicing telling time from this clock, children can use the index cards to reinforce how the numbers relate to the time.

⊚ Sit in a circle and practice going around the circle, counting by fives to 55. For more fun, toss a beach ball to random students around the circle, having each child say the next number as he or she catches the ball.

⊚ Play a matching game. Give half the class cards with clock numbers (1–12) written in black and the other half cards with the corresponding minutes (5, 10, 15, 20, 25, and so on.) written in red. Have students find their match.

Eileen Delfini
Richboro Elementary School
Richboro, Pennsylvania

Lakeshore Learning (**www.lakeshore learning.com**) offers a large assortment of clocks with moveable hands, working cash registers, plastic coins, and other materials for teaching time.

Literature LINK

Clocks and More Clocks

by Pat Hutchins (Aladdin, 1994)

This funny picture book tells the story of Mr. Higgins and his clocks. Mr. Higgins keeps buying more and more clocks to find out which one is telling the correct time. He races around his house from room to room, always finding each clock to be a few minutes behind the other. It's not until a wise clock maker shows Mr. Higgins his errors that he rests.

Time Expressions

Bring language arts into your math lessons by exploring expressions of time.

- Challenge students to listen for expressions about time. For example, children might hear the expressions *time flies; time stands still; there aren't not enough hours in the day; a stitch in time saves nine; the early bird catches the worm; early to bed, early to rise makes a man healthy, wealthy, and wise; time-out; time's a wasting; behind the times; in good time; time on your hands; time of your life; time after time;* and *high time.*

- Invite children to record these expressions in a class learning log and share them with the class. Take time to read them aloud with the class.

- As an extension, have children create an illustrated collaborative banner of their time expressions. Ask each child to choose an expression. Have children write their expressions on sheets of drawing paper and then illustrate them. Arrange the illustrations side by side on a long sheet of roll paper. Glue or tape them in place and display in the hallway for others to enjoy.

What do A.M. and P.M. stand for? Share with students that A.M. is Latin for *ante meridiem*, which means before midday. The initials P.M.. stand for *post meridiem*, which means after midday.

Literature
LINK

It's About Time!

selected by Lee Bennett Hopkins (Simon & Schuster, 1993)

Poems by Aileen Fisher, Gwendolyn Brooks, Jack Prelutsky, Charlotte Zolotow, and others fill the pages of this delightful collection of poetry. Charming illustrations capture each hour of a child's day—from waking up "wound" like a clock to thinking bedtime thoughts. Clocks in the upper corner of each page reinforce the concept of passing time.

Experiment with varying the size of the holes students punch in the paper. Have students compare the elapsed time for each. How does the size of the hole change the amount of time it takes for the sand to run through?

Make a Timer

With just a few simple materials, students become clock makers to learn about units of time.

- Gather the following materials to make the clocks: plastic liter soda bottles (two per student or team), heavy paper, hole punch, duct tape, sand or salt.

- Ask students to trace the mouth of one bottle on the paper, then cut out the circle and carefully punch a hole in the center of it.

- Have students pour sand or salt into one bottle, filling it almost to the top. Have them put the paper circle over the mouth of this bottle and place the mouth of the other bottle on top. Have students tape the two bottles together. (If children each make a timer, have them help each other with this step. One child can hold the bottles in place while the other tapes them together.)

- On your signal, have students turn their clocks upside-down and time how long it takes the salt to run through to the other jar.

- Let students use their clocks to time each other in fun tasks—for example, how many jumping jacks can they do in the time it takes for the sand to run through?

Bob Krech
Dutch Neck Elementary School
Princeton Junction, New Jersey

Shadow Math

Take advantage of a clear, sunny day to let students turn their shadows into a sundial!

As early in the morning as possible, preferably at the top of the hour, take children outside to a safe, clear paved area, such as a section of the playground or a school sidewalk. Before proceeding, caution children not to look directly at the sun as this could harm their eyes. Have students line up side by side, and give every other child a piece of sidewalk chalk. Have the children with the chalk trace a neighboring classmate's shadow and then trade places so that each child's shadow gets traced. Have children record their name and the time at the top of their shadows. At the passing of each hour, return to the shadow outlines to trace the top of each student's new shadow and record the time. Invite students to discuss the lengths and times before and after noon. What patterns do they notice?

Time Around the World

After sharing books about time zones (see Literature Link, below), invite students to explore geography by finding out the time in different parts of the world.

Display a world map and use sticky notes to mark time zones. Start by asking children what time it is somewhere in the world—for example, if you're in New York and it's 10 A.M., what time is it in California? Have a student use the map to determine the answer, then let this child ask the next question. Continue until you've covered all the time zones and plenty of times.

Jackie Clarke
Cicero Elementary School
Cicero, New York

Find the exact times in cities around the world at Time and Date.com: **www.timeand date.com/world clock**. This site also allows you to check sunrise and sunset times around the world and compare a selected city's time to other time zones!

Literature LINK

Somewhere in the World Right Now

by Stacey Schuett (Dragonfly, 1997)

This picture book is a great way to introduce the concept of time zones. It is full of maps, beautiful illustrations, and easy-to-read interesting text. It follows activities occurring simultaneously around the world in different time zones. *Nine O'Clock Lullaby,* by Marilyn Singer (Harper Trophy, 1993), offers a more lyrical look at time zones. A rhythmic lullaby lets readers "travel" through the different time zones to see what's going on around the world when it is 9:00 P.M. in New York, including the mid-Atlantic at midnight, England at 2 A.M., and Australia at noon.

Sundial Time-Tellers

Have students see how a real sundial works by building this class model. You'll need a sheet of white tagboard, a nail, and a pen.

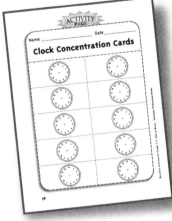

At the start of a school day, place a sheet of tagboard on the ground outside in sunny spot. Use a few small rocks to hold the tagboard in place. Poke a long nail through the center of the tagboard. Make sure you leave most of the nail showing. (You might use a small bit of clay at the base of the nail to add stability.) Mark the tip of the nail's shadow with a line, and record the time. Repeat this procedure each hour, marking the tip of the shadow and recording the time. Let children use the sundial the next day to tell time. For a challenge, have them estimate the time when the shadow falls somewhere between the lines they've marked. Compare their estimates with the actual time. Let students try again later. Are their estimates closer this time?

Clock Concentration

A fun way for kids to practice matching digital times with analog clocks is this game of Concentration.

Make one copy of the reproducible cards on pages 38 and 39. Complete the cards by filling in matching times on the digital and analog clock cards, then make multiple copies of each. Divide the class into small groups and give each a set of cards (one from each page). Have children cut apart the cards, mix them up, and place them facedown. Have players take turns turning over two cards to see if they match. If a player gets a matching analog and digital clock card, he or she takes the cards. If not, the cards are turned facedown again and the next player takes a turn. Play until all cards have been matched.

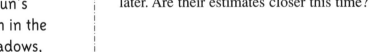

Help introduce the concept of the sun's position in the sky, shadows, and how sundials work, with "Shadow Race," a poem by Shel Silverstein from *A Light in the Attic* (HarperCollins, 1981).

Kid Clocks

This lively activity invites students to become the parts of a clock as they practice telling time.

- Review the parts of the clock (numbers, hands, circle shape). Write the numbers 1 to 12 on large index cards (one number per card) and give one to each of 12 children.

- Have these children arrange themselves in a large circle. Invite two volunteers to be the hour and minute hands of the clock. Have one lie inside the circle with feet placed at the center of the circle and hands stretched out over his or her head to be the minute hand. Have the other lie inside the circle (again with feet at the center of the circle) with arms at the side to be the hour hand.

- Let the remaining students take turns calling out a time and helping the "clock hands" get into position. After changing the time several times, let students trade places so that they can all be a clock part.

- Turn the clock number index cards over and write the corresponding Roman numerals. Use the cards to make a "kid clock" with a Roman numeral clock face.

Rock Around the Clock

Help children learn about elapsed time with an activity that combines math, music, and movement. You'll need a clock with moveable hands, a CD or tape player, and some lively music.

To help students understand elapsed time, teach them to first count the hours that have passed and then add on the minutes.

Set the clock to a particular time. Have students record the time on a sheet of paper. Invite a student to stand up in front of the class and hold the clock so that everyone can see it. Start the music while the volunteer slowly pushes the hands around the clock. Kids may move around or dance in their places while the music plays. When you stop the music, have the child holding the clock stop moving the hands. Have the other children sit down. Ask students to figure out how much time has passed on the clock. After discussing the results, repeat the activity, letting another student hold the clock and move the hands.

Tissue-Box Time Lines

Here's an easy way for students to create a three-dimensional time line about their day.

⊚ Give each student white construction paper, markers or crayons, and a square tissue box. Have students trace one of the upright sides of the tissue box onto the construction paper, cut it out, then use it as a template to cut out three additional squares.

⊚ Ask students to think about four different activities they do in one day—for example, get on the bus, have recess, eat lunch, and go to bed. Invite them to write about and illustrate each activity on the four squares of paper, then record the time of the day they usually do the activity.

⊚ Have students glue the four papers in order to the sides of the box. Give students time to compare their activities and the times they do them.

A.M. - P.M. Flip Book

Make these fun books to strengthen students' understanding of the differences between A.M. and P.M.

⊚ Have students fold a sheet of paper in half (vertically), then turn the paper horizontally (with the fold at the top) and cut two slits, as shown, to divide the front flap into thirds.

⊚ Ask students to choose a favorite morning activity and to illustrate it on the front of the first flap. Have them write the time (including A.M.) on the flap. Have students repeat this procedure to complete the front of the other two flaps—illustrating a favorite morning activity and recording the A.M. time.

⊚ Have students do the same under each flap, this time illustrating three favorite afternoon or evening activities. Have them record the time for each, being sure to add P.M.

⊚ Invite students to share their flip books with one another, comparing favorite activities and times that they do them.

Peg Arcadi
Homeschool Teacher
Trumansburg, New York

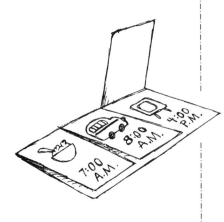

TIP

As a variation, invite students to choose an activity that goes with each of four months. Have them illustrate the activities on the tissue-box time lines (in order) and write the name of the month on each corresponding side.

How Long Will It Take?

How long does it really take a minute to pass by? Discuss with students how long a minute is (60 seconds). Then try this activity to reinforce the concept of time and strengthen subtraction skills, too.

Have children count to 60 to get a feel for how long 60 seconds lasts. Next, ask students how many things they think they can do in a minute—for example, how many times they can write their names, snap their fingers, hop, do jumping jacks, tie their sneakers, and say the alphabet. List ideas on the chalkboard. Give each child a copy of page 36. In the first box, have students record an estimate of what they can do in one minute. Pair up students and give them a stopwatch. While one partner tries the activity, have the other partner time a minute on the stopwatch. After completing the activity, ask students to calculate the differences between what they thought they could do in a minute and what they actually did. Have students use the remaining boxes to estimate and try out two additional one-minute activities.

Wendy Wise-Borg
Maurice Hawk Elementary School
Princeton Junction, New Jersey

Dear Benjamin Banneker

by Andrea Davis Pinkney (Voyager, 1998)

This beautifully illustrated picture-book biography about Benjamin Banneker is a great introduction to the first African American to write and publish an almanac. His almanacs were full of accurate calendars. He also was famous in his day for making a wooden striking clock that kept accurate time for more than 50 years—one of the first and finest wooden clocks made in Colonial America! This history maker was also an astronomer, a farmer, a surveyor, and a mathematician!

To obtain an informal assessment of students' understanding, post a time that includes the notation of A.M. or P.M. Ask students to copy the time on a sheet of paper and draw a picture of an activity they might perform at that time.

Calendar Clues

Invite your students to become number detectives while trying to figure out a secret date on the calendar.

Before starting, come up with a set of number clues that correspond to dates on the calendar—for example, "This number is equal to half a dozen" or "This number is half the number of students in our class." Hide the clues under dates on the classroom calendar, being sure to place them so that one clue will lead to the next. (You can use sticky notes to make flaps on the calendar squares. Write the clues under the flaps.) Under the last flap, write a surprise that students will get—for example, an extra recess or free-reading time. Come up with a separate clue that will lead students to the first flap—for example, "This is the number of inches in a foot." (This clue will lead students to the number 12, under which they'll find the next clue.) Let students take turns solving clues until they get to the secret date, where they'll find their surprise!

Save That Date

Invite students to explore each month of the year by having them talk with family members at home about important dates to remember.

Make copies of Save That Date, a reproducible monthly calendar. (See page 40.) Have students take the calendar home and discuss with their families dates that are important in each month—for example, family birthdays, holidays, and so on. Ask students to write the dates in the boxes and draw a picture that symbolizes the activity, person, holiday, or event. that makes this date important.

When is International Joke Day? How about Amelia Earhart's birthday or National Dog Week? Find out when these and other dates fall at Surfing the Net with Kids: **www. surfnetkids.com /sept.htm**, where you'll find listings and facts for just about every day of the year!

Round and Round Clock Rhyme

Use the following rhyme during transition times or as a warm-up activity to reinforce telling time.

Have students get their notebooks out, or supply them with lined paper. Using a clock with moveable hands, recite the following rhyme while moving the hands around and around. Stop the hands when you get to the end of the rhyme.

> **Round and round and round it goes,**
> **Where it stops, nobody knows,**
> **Where it stops will be the time,**
> **Write the time on the very next line!**

Have children record the time shown on the clock, being sure to add A.M. or P.M. if this is a focus of your time-telling lessons. This is a great way to keep kids engaged while doing rote practice. When students get the hang of it, let them take turns moving the clock hands as they lead the class in the rhyme.

Barbara Gauker
Immaculate Conception School
Bristol, Pennsylvania

Literature LINK

The Grouchy Ladybug

by Eric Carle (HarperCollins, 1996)

This classic picture book was first published more than 20 years ago, but it remains a timeless piece of literature that students will remember from younger days. The colorful die-cut pages follow the story of a grouchy ladybug as she picks a fight with increasingly larger animals. A clock face at the top of each page lets children track the passing of time as the suspense in the story builds. As a followup, let children write a collaborative story about their day, using a clock face on each page to show the passing of time.

TIP

Invite your students to travel back in time to learn about timekeeping practices of the past. A Walk Through Time (**physics.nist.gov/GenInt/Time/time.html**) features ancient calendars and early clocks and includes several examples of interesting and strange time-keeping devices.

Comparing Clocks

Students are so often used to seeing digital clocks in their world that it can be extra confusing for them to learn how to tell time with analog clocks. Use a Venn diagram to help them see similarities and differences between the two types of clocks.

Divide the class into groups. Give some groups a working analog clock and others a working digital clock. Give groups with the analog clocks circle-shaped cards, and those with digital clocks rectangle-shaped cards. Ask students to examine their clocks and to record their features on the index cards (one feature per card). Bring students together to share the cards. Make a Venn diagram to learn more. Draw two large overlapping circles. Label one circle "Analog" and one "Digital." Let children take turns placing their cards in the appropriate circles, indicating whether the features apply to one or both clocks. Discuss the results: How are the clocks alike? How are they different?

Invite students to bring in and share extra clocks from home, including alarm clocks, digital clocks, clocks with Roman numerals, clocks without numbers, watches, and so on.

Time Check!

This activity strengthens students' time-telling abilities and provides a quick and easy informal assessment.

Give each student a copy of the record sheets on page 41. Have children tape one of the record sheets to their desks. Model the activity by announcing that it's time for a "time check." Check the clock, tell the time, and write it on the chalkboard. Have children write the time on their papers, too. At selected times throughout the school day, ring a bell or announce that it is a "time check" moment. Have students stop what they're doing, look at the classroom analog clock, and record the time. Keep a master for your records. Collect the sheets at the end of the day or when all the spaces have been filled. Check students' records against your own for assessment purposes. As students' abilities grow, ask questions about elapsed time—for example, "How many more minutes until we go to art? How long has it been since the last time check?"

Stacey Brandes
St. Joseph School
Burlington, Vermont

Stories Tell Time

Using literature to teach math concepts helps students to make connections, enjoy literature, and view math in a different way.

Divide the class into groups. Give each group a book that relates to time in some way—for example, *The Very Hungry Caterpillar,* by Eric Carle (Philomel, 1969), is a classic for teaching days of the week. Other concepts to cover include hours, months, seasons, elapsed time, and schedules. (See Literature Links throughout this book for suggested titles.) Invite students in each group to share the book among themselves and then brainstorm ways the book teaches about time. Let each group prepare a book-based mini-lesson about that concept. (Model a mini-lesson first and discuss lesson formats students might use.) These mini-lessons lead to lots of creative thinking, and students love playing the part of teacher.

Bobbie Williams
Brookwood Elementary School
Snellville, Georgia

Take-Home Activity: Family Planner

With today's busy families, a planner is always helpful for organizing family events and activities. Help students practice using time schedules as they work together with their families to plan out a week of activities and events.

Make copies of the reproducible daily planner on page 42. Have students take home the planner and complete it with their families for the following week. Families can post the planner on refrigerators or another handy spot and refer to it as they plan their time. Ask students to bring the planners back to school after the week is over. Discuss similarities and differences in schedules—for example, How many students noted doctor's appointments on their schedules? Soccer practice? Meetings? Special occasions?

Make a Theme Clock

Celebrate your study of time by having children design clocks that connect with their own interests and hobbies.

- Share with students magazine and catalog pictures of unique clocks and watches. Discuss the various hobbies and interests the clocks might represent—for example, a bird lover might appreciate a clock with pictures of birds that also chirps their songs on the hour.

- Have students write down a couple of interests or hobbies on a sheet of paper. Under each topic, have students make a list of picture ideas that match their topic—for example, balls that represent favorite sports, or different kinds of pets for an animal lover.

- Have students use the reproducible clock face (see page 43) to create a clock with their hobby or interest as a theme. Make a checklist on the chalkboard to remind students of the features, including hands, 5-minute symbols, and marks for minutes.

- Invite students to arrange their clocks on a bulletin board and to come up with a name for their display.

Visit the Official Source of Time for the Department of Defense and the Standard Time for the United States at: **tycho.usno. navy.mil/**.

Literature LINK

A Quarter From the Tooth Fairy

by Caren Holtzman (Scholastic, 1995)

This easy reader tells the story of a boy who receives a quarter from the Tooth Fairy. He thinks about all the things he can buy for twenty-five cents, but gets so confused that he decides to buy his tooth back.

Money Word Wall

Kick off a study of money by building a word wall that will help you assess what students already know and serve as a teaching tool for more learning.

Invite students to call out words associated with money—for example, *cash, dollar, cents, value, bank, pay, save, hundred, quarter, nickel, coins, pennies, dimes, nickels, half-dollars*. Write the words on tagboard shapes that represent money (for example, rectangular dollar-bill shapes and circular coin shapes). Display the word cards at children's eye level. Keep blank word cards handy so that students can add to the word wall as they learn more about money. Use the word wall as a source of skill-building games—for example:

⑤ Strengthen spelling by starting to spell a "mystery word" on the word wall. Say each letter slowly, letting children take turns spelling the rest of the word as soon as they discover which one it is.

⑤ Build concepts by letting children sort the word cards. (If you attach them with Velcro "hook and eye" fasteners, they'll be easy to put up and take down.) You might start a sorting pattern—for example, grouping cards by words that name values (quarter, dollar, and so on.) and words that don't—then let children come up one at a time to add a word to a group.

⑤ Let students take turns reading the words in alphabetical order. Use words that start with the same letter—for example, *cash* and *cents*—as the focus of a mini-lesson to learn more about alphabetizing.

Someone who collects coins is called a numismatic. Conduct a class survey to find out what students collect.

SECOND Language LEARNERS

Strengthen students' understanding of the word *change* by discussing the multiple meanings of the word. Show students the word as a verb in the sentence: "Can you change a 5 dollar bill for 5 ones?" Show students the word as a noun in the sentence "The change in my pocket is gone!" Show students the word as another noun in the sentence "How much change do I get?" Let students brainstorm other words with more than one usage—for example, *saw, present,* and *can.*

Money Around the World

Introduce students to currencies around the world with this fun fact: The smallest money ever used was the Greek *obelas*. It was smaller than an apple seed. People kept the obelas in their mouths, hoping they wouldn't sneeze or swallow! Learn more about money around the world with an activity that integrates math with geography, literature, and the Internet.

⊚ Invite students to bring in from home any coins their families might have from other countries. Let students share their coins and the names for them if they know them. Use the information on this page (see Tip, left) to introduce the names of other currencies around the world.

⊚ After learning the names of some of the different currencies, share *Money,* by Joe Cribb (Dorling Kindersley, 2000), a book of photos and fun facts about the history of money. Encourage students to look for photos that correspond to any of the coins they brought in. Share interesting information about these coins.

⊚ For more fun, visit Web sites that show currency conversions. Challenge children to find out what it would cost to buy, for example, a school lunch in other countries. Start with countries represented by coins children shared from home. Two Web sites to try are 164 Currency Converter by OANDA (**www.oanda.com/cgi-bin/ncc**) and Universal Currency Converter (**www.xe.net/ucc**).

Some of the world's currencies:

China: yuan
France: franc
Germany: euro
Greece: drachna
India: rupee
Italy: lira
Japan: yen
Mexico: peso
Spain: peseta

SECOND Language LEARNERS

Use a lesson on world currency to build bridges between your second-language learners' countries of origin and what they're learning in class. Invite children to create a poster that features their country's currency. Have them include words for coins, bills, and so on. Display the poster next to one that shows the currency they're learning about. Make comparisons: Are the coins a similar size? How do their values differ?

Let's Make Change

Students practice making change with this musical role-playing activity.

🌀 Divide the class into pairs. Assign students the role of buyer or seller. Supply the sellers with resealable bags filled with $3.00 worth of plastic coins. Supply the buyers with resealable bags containing several green sheets of construction paper cut to the size of dollar bills.

🌀 Invite the sellers to choose three items (for example, a pencil, marker, and eraser) from their desks that they would like to sell. Have them use sticky notes (with their names) to put a price on each item (less than one dollar). Then have sellers display the items on their desks.

🌀 When sellers are ready, have buyers line up in front of their desks. Play some music and have the buyers move from one desk to the next. When you stop the music, buyers stop and purchase something at the nearest desk. The seller must give the buyer correct change.

🌀 Have students switch roles and money bags after taking several turns. Remind students that all items will be returned after the activity.

Becky Mandia
Newtown Elementary
Newtown, Pennsylvania

Literature
LINK

My Rows and Piles of Coins

by Tololwa M. Mollel (Clarion, 1999)

This award-winning picture book tells the story of an African boy named Saruni. Saruni dreams of buying a bicycle and saves all his coins for months and months, but he discovers he does not have enough. Saruni is assisted by his father and in return begins saving to help his family by a cart. An author's note at the end describes some of the African coins featured in the story and their values in relation to other coins.

Strengthen students' coin-counting abilities with the software program *Coin Critters* (Nordic Software). Students practice distinguishing between U.S. coins, matching coins, and counting change.

Book Orders Add Up

Classroom book orders provide a great way for students to practice using money in real-life situations. Use your book order forms with the following activities:

- Have students select several books they would like to have, record them on the order form, and use paper and pencil or a calculator to add up their purchases. (Make additional copies so that students can use the forms for actual orders as well as for fun and practice.)

- Give students a set amount they can "spend." Challenge them to see who can get the most books for that amount of money.

- Have students put the books in order from highest to lowest price.

- Create word problems using students' names—for example, "Mick and Lucy each have three dollars. They want to combine their money to buy and share books. What are some book combinations they can buy?"

- Incorporate literature by inviting students to add up the number of books in the same genre, on the same subject, by the same author, and so on.

TIP

Share with students the fact that paper money was first issued in the United States on March 10, 1862, and became legal tender by an act of Congress seven days later.

Literature LINK

Benny's Pennies
by Pat Brisson (Yearling, 1995)

A boy named Benny has five new pennies—and five different ways to spend them. Will he be able to buy all five things? This cumulative story is a great read-aloud and teaches a lesson not only about the value of pennies but of spending wisely.

Money Makes History

Why are certain people from history honored by having their face on United States currency? Encourage students to find out by learning about the lives of people depicted on U.S. coins and bills.

Invite students to team up to research someone pictured on a coin or bill. Encourage students to find out why they think that person was chosen. Challenge students to present their information to the class in a novel way: Have students create a poster-size illustration of the coin or bill they researched. Show them how to cut out the center of the coin or bill to make room for their heads to peek through. Let students present their biographical information in the first person—for example, "I am Sacagawea and I am pictured on the new dollar. I helped Lewis and Clark on their expedition out west…" Children in each group can take a turn being the face on the coin or bill and sharing information.

Literature LINK

Alexander, Who Used to Be Rich Last Sunday

by Judith Viorst (Aladdin, 1980)

This classic picture book describes the story of Alexander, who received a dollar from his grandparents one weekend. Little by little the money disappears as he spends some on bubble gum, rents a snake for an hour, and gets fined by his dad, among other things. Invite your students to interact with the story as you read it aloud. Supply each student with seven dimes, four nickels, and ten pennies. As students hear about Alexander losing a specific amount of money, have them take away the matching amount from their piles. For a challenge, invite students to count and write the amount of money he has at different stages of the story.

TIP

Learn about the history of money at **www.wdfi.org /ymm/kids/ history/default. asp**. You'll also find quizzes, pictures of money, and links to related sites.

Design a Coin

Children learn about the features of coins by designing their own!

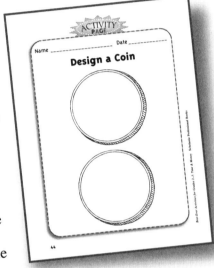

Make copies of the reproducible coin templates on page 44. Review the parts of a coin by having students take a close look at real coins. What do they have in common? How are they different? Let students sketch their coin designs first, determining the value, symbols, color, and words to appear on the front and back. They can transfer their designs to the templates, cut out the coins, and glue the front and back together (back sides together). Let students write about the features of their coins on a separate sheet of paper. Do their coins feature a person or place? Does the coin represent a value other than that of an existing coin? Display the coins by punching a hole through the top and pulling string through to hang from the classroom ceiling. Display the descriptions on a bulletin board so that readers can look up to find the matching coins.

State by State

Get your students excited about United States geography and money at the same time.

Gather as many different state quarters as you can and place them in a jar. Organize students into groups of three or four. Invite each group to pick a quarter from the jar. Have students research their group's quarter to find out more about the symbolism of the picture on the back and learn some fun and interesting facts about that state. Have each group create a presentation about the coin and the state it represents.

Mitzi Fehl
Poquoson Primary school
Poquoson, Virginia

Visit the Official United States Mint Web site (**www.usmint. gov**) for information about the U.S. State Quarter Program. For states that have not released their quarters or announced their symbol, invite students to research the state and select a fitting state symbol.

Poetry Money Math

Share a thought-provoking poem to help children understand that more coins don't always equal more money. Then play a fast-paced game to learn more.

⊚ Read aloud Shel Silverstein's poem "Smart," from *Where the Sidewalk Ends*. (See Literature Link, below.) As they listen, ask children to think about each trade the boy makes. For example, when he trades a dollar bill for two shiny quarters, is he making a "smart" trade? Why?

⊚ Let children share their thoughts about each trade in the poem. Then have them team up with partners to write new verses. Reread the poem, substituting students' lines for original verses. Again, discuss whether or not the trades are "smart."

⊚ Follow up by letting students play Rolling for Coins, a game that reinforces concepts about money. Give pairs of children two copies of the record sheet (see page 45), a die, and a bag of assorted coins. Have children take turns rolling the die and taking the corresponding number of coins from the bag (without looking). Have children count up the value of the coins and record both the number of coins and their value on the record sheet. For each round, have students circle the highest number rolled and put a square around the highest value.

⊚ After letting children play several rounds, bring them together for a discussion. Does the highest number rolled always result in more coins? (*Yes*) Does this always result in more money? (*No*)

Literature
LINK

Where the Sidewalk Ends

by Shel Silverstein (HarperCollins, 1974)

What would your students say if someone offered to trade them two shiny dimes for one quarter? Share the poem "Smart" to challenge your students' thinking problems like this. In the poem, a child thinks he is really smart because he trades one quarter for two shiny dimes (because two is more than one), two dimes for three nickels (because three is more than two), and so on.

The software program *Dollarville* (Waypoint Software) is divided into four levels of difficulty and provides students with opportunities to learn all about money. A character named Deputy Dollar guides students through the game.

Visit Ron's Currency, Stocks, and Bonds at **www.ronscur rency.com/rhist. htm** to see a time line of the history of paper money in the United States. Find out answers to the following questions: Which bank was the first to issue paper money? When did "In God We Trust" first appear on paper money?

Coupon Clippers

Here's an easy game to play that uses coupons to strengthen students' skills in comparing different amounts of money.

- Collect newspaper coupon circulars. Have students bring some in from home, too. Cut out the coupons as they come in. You'll need about 20 per child.

- When you have enough coupons, divide the class into pairs and give each child a set of coupons. Have children shuffle their coupons and stack them facedown.

- To play, have both players place the coupon on top faceup at the same time. The player with the higher money amount on his or her coupon takes both. If the value of the coupons turned over is the same, have children turn over another coupon, continuing until one is higher than the other. The player with the higher value takes all the coupons from that round.

- Play continues until all coupons have been turned over and taken. The player with the most coupons wins. As a followup, invite students to work together to arrange the coupons in order from least value to greatest value.

Literature LINK

Coin County: A Bank in a Book

by Jim Talbot (Innovative Kids, 1999)

Get children excited about saving money with this interactive picture book. It's told in rhyme and covers the many ways that coins add up to a dollar. Children can save more than $20.00 by filling the coin slots built into each page. With slots for pennies, nickels, dimes, and quarters, students can practice counting with real money. (This might make a fun class project; students can choose a charity to donate their coins to when they've filled all of the slots.)

Counting Coins Clapping

When counting coins, children must be able to count by ones, fives, tens, and twenty-fives. Let them practice counting by these numbers with an activity that engages their kinesthetic learning styles.

- Gather enough real or plastic quarters, dimes, and nickels to count to 50 with each (two quarters, five dimes, and ten nickels).

- Call out the number 50. As you drop two quarters in a container, have students call out the value and clap the number of quarters. *(25, 50, clap twice)*

- Repeat the procedure for dimes, having students count and clap each group of ten. Now try nickels. Each time, help students make the connection between smaller value coins and larger value coins.

Literature
LINK

The Coin Counting Book

by Rozanne Lanczak Williams (Charlesbridge, 2001)

"One penny, two pennies, three pennies, four. What will we get when we add just one more?" That's the way this book of verse begins. Full of color photos of coins, this book introduces the counting of coins all the way up to the new Sacagawea dollar!

TiP

When students are well-practiced in counting by these numbers, try mixing it up. Count to 50 using dimes and nickels. (Have them watch closely to see which coin you are dropping in the container.) Add some pennies to the combinations, too.

 **Pocket Change**

Get your students excited about counting change and familiarize them with coin characteristics at the same time.

⊙ Give each child a copy of the reproducible activity sheet on page 46, some coins, and a crayon.

⊙ Ask children to hide some of the coins in the pocket (placing the coins under the paper and making sure they are inside the outline of the pocket).

⊙ Have children trade seats, leaving their papers and hidden coins on the desks. Once children are seated, ask them to estimate the amount of change in the pocket by feeling the coins through the paper. Then have them record their estimates in the space provided, being careful not to move the coins.

⊙ Invite children to use the crayons to make a colorful rubbing of the hidden coins. Ask them to revise their estimates if they wish (based on the rubbings). Then have them lift the paper to reveal the hidden coins and record the actual amount of change in the pocket. Use the rubbings to create a colorful display that reinforces coin values and characteristics.

Coins Weigh In

Strengthen familiarity with coins and counting skills with an activity that invites children to measure weights.

When teaching children how to count change, remind them to first group like coins together and then arrange them from greatest to least value.

Set up a learning station with several balances and containers of quarters, dimes, nickels, and pennies. To model the activity, ask students to predict how many dimes it will take to balance the scale with one penny. Try it out and discuss the results, reviewing both the number of dimes it took and the value—for example, it took two dimes, or 20 cents worth of dimes, to equal one penny. Set up a chart to record information, providing space to record predictions and results. Let students visit the station in small groups to test out more combinations, recording their predictions and results on the chart.

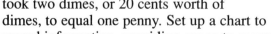

Colonial Money Word Problems

In colonial times the units of money were called shillings and pounds. Try this activity to have some fun with this system of currency.

○ Begin, if possible, by sharing *What Are You Figuring Now? A Story About Benjamin Banneker.* (See below.) Review one of Banneker's word problems that appears in the book: "A gentleman sent his servant 100 pounds to buy cattle (bullocks and cows) and sheep, with orders to give 5 pounds for each bullock, 20 shillings worth of cows, and 1 shilling for each sheep. What number of each sort did he buy for his master?"

○ Explain to students that 20 shillings equals one pound, then let them team up to solve the problem. Have students share their solutions and the reasoning behind them. (*The answer is 19 bullocks at 5 pounds each = 95 pounds; 1 cow at 20 shillings = 1 pound; 80 sheep at 1 shilling each = 4 pounds.*)

○ Then let students create their own math word problems using shillings and pounds. Have students trade papers and solve each other's problems. Or use them to create a display. Students can solve the problems as they have time, recording their work and answers on a record sheet.

TIP

Share with students that throughout history there have been all kinds of funny things used as money, including shells, salt, grain, cloth, animals, tools, feathers, belts of beads, and fruit. Ask students to compare these old forms with today's currencies.

Literature LINK

What Are You Figuring Now? A Story About Benjamin Banneker

by Jeri Ferris (Carolrhoda, 1988)

This easy reader about Benjamin Banneker gives more details about this great African-American mathematician's life—including how he loved to make difficult math word problems involving money. Try the activity above to strengthen students' own skills with writing and solving money word problems.

On the Money

Strengthen students' familiarity with coins while improving their counting skills, too.

Invite students to create number sentences using the historical figures on different United States coins. For example: 2 Lincolns + 5 Jeffersons = 27 cents. Students can write their number sentences on colorful sentence strips, then hide the answer under a sticky note or construction paper flap and draw a question mark on it. Display the sentence strips along with pictures of each coin. Let children solve each other's equations, using the pictures to determine the value of the coins. To take students' explorations further, have them complete the chart on page 47, using real coins for reference.

Sue Lorey
Grove Avenue School
Barrington, Illinois

Did you ever wonder what type of cars are on the back of a ten-dollar bill or which states appear on the back of a five-dollar bill? Find out the answers to these questions and more at the Department of the Treasury's Web site at **www.treas. gov/opc/opcoo 34.html**.

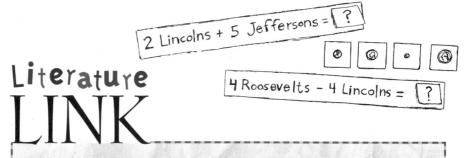

2 Lincolns + 5 Jeffersons = ?

4 Roosevelts - 4 Lincolns = ?

Literature LINK

If You Made a Million
by David M. Schwartz (Mulberry Books, 1994)

In this sequel to *How Much Is a Million?* the Mathematical Magician and his friends begin to wonder about things like how high a stack of $100 worth of pennies would be. Wacky illustrations show the answers. The characters also travel to a bank and learn about grown-up things like interest, checking accounts, loans, and income tax. To learn more about the concept of a million, try the activities in *The Magic of a Million Activity Book*, by David M. Schwartz and David J. Whitin (Scholastic, 1998). Cross-curricular hands-on activities and ready-to-reproduce data collection sheets help make big numbers exciting and concrete, while providing practice in skills such as estimating, counting, calculating, measuring, and more.

Money Match

Turn coin-counting practice into a game with this easy idea.

Let students pair up with a classmate to play this game. Give each player a set of plastic coins that includes multiple half-dollars, quarters, dimes, nickels, and pennies. Have players take turns choosing and displaying an amount of money under $1.00. The other player needs to match the amount of money, using a different combination of coins.

Make a Date With Money

Add a pink construction paper piggy bank to your class calendar to set up for some practice with coins and bills.

Place real or plastic money (including pennies, nickels, dimes, quarters, half-dollar, and dollar bills) in clear contact paper squares, leaving a space at the top for punching a hole. Stack the coins by value, and use straight pins to hang on a bulletin board with the class calendar. Each day, invite a child to select money with a value equal to the day's date—for example, if it's the third day of the month, the child will select three pennies. Have the child use straight pins to attach the money to the piggy bank. When the date gets to the fifth of the month, the pennies have to be exchanged for a nickel, and so on, up to the dollar bill. Students love doing this and it teaches a lot about the value of the coins and provides practice with exchanging coins.

Judy Meagher
Student Teacher Supervisor
Bozeman, Montana

Display an assortment of coins on an overhead. Make sure the total value can be represented by another combination of fewer coins. For example, show three nickels and five pennies. Ask students to draw coins on paper (or use plastic coins) to show the same value using the fewest coins possible—for example, instead of three nickels and five pennies, they could use two dimes.

TIP

Use the book *Math for Smarty Pants,* by Marilyn Burns (Little Brown, 1982), to enrich your lessons on money. Activities include, Money Alphabet, in which a monetary value is assigned to each letter of the alphabet. Children will love exploring the value of their names.

Calculating Classmates

Students will have fun combining and adding coins while playing this game with their classmates.

Obtain oversized coins from a teacher supply store or create them yourself. Attach string to each coin to make a necklace. Give each student a coin necklace. Play music while students walk around the classroom. When the music stops, have each student find a partner and sit down. Ask partners to calculate their totals. Have partners share their totals with the class to check for accuracy. Play again, repeating the procedure but making the game more challenging by giving each child more than one necklace. Or, when the music stops, have children form groups of three or four, then calculate their totals.

Literature LINK

A Dollar for Penny

by Dr. Julie Glass (Random House, 2000)

In this rhyming easy reader, a girl named Penny opens a lemonade stand, and watches her earnings add up to a dollar. A table of coins and values appear at the back.

SECOND Language LEARNERS

Make a money reference tool for second-language learners by creating a chart with three columns labeled "Coin," "Name," and "Value." Give children pictures of coins (or plastic coins) to glue in the first column of the chart. Have them complete the chart by recording the names of the coins and their values. Let them attach the charts to their desks for easy reference.

Take-Home Activity:
Counting and Comparing Coins

The riddles on page 48 let families work together to learn more about money.

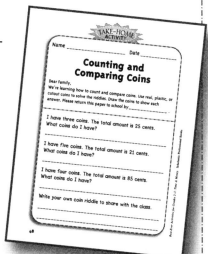

Give each child a copy of page 48. Review the page, making sure children know that these are riddles they can solve with a family member. Have children notice that there are three riddles on the page, plus space for creating a new riddle to share with the class. When children return their papers to class, compile their new riddles. Use them to create new take-home activity pages for reinforcing money skills and concepts!

Guess My Coin Combination

Children always enjoy a good guessing game. This fun and challenging game for partners will strengthen students' skills in using different combinations of coins to count to a specific amount.

Students will need sticky notes, pencils, and an assortment of real or plastic quarters, dimes, nickels, and pennies. The first player writes an amount that is less than $1.00 and records a combination of coins that equal that amount, then covers the amount and combination with a sticky note. The first player tells the second player the hidden amount and how many coins make up the secret coin combination. The second player tries to guess and show the correct combination.

When teaching children to count coins, remind them to group like coins together. Try to start with the coin with the highest value, then the next highest, and so on. This comes in handy for purchasing something with the fewest number of coins.

Name _____ Date _____

How Long Will It Take?

Activity: _____

Estimate	Actual

Activity: _____

Estimate	Actual

Activity: _____

Estimate	Actual

Shadow Math

Activity: _____

Activity: _____

Activity: _____

Activity: _____

Name _____ Date _____

Clock Concentration Cards

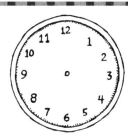

Best-Ever Activities for Grades 2–3: Time & Money   Scholastic Professional Books

Name _____   Date _____

Clock Concentration Cards

_____ : _____   _____ : _____

_____ : _____   _____ : _____

_____ : _____   _____ : _____

_____ : _____   _____ : _____

_____ : _____   _____ : _____

Name _____   Date _____

Save That Date

Practice reading a calendar with family members, and find out some dates that are important enough to save.

January	February	March

April	May	June

July	August	September

October	November	December

Best-Ever Activities for Grades 2–3: Time & Money Scholastic Professional Books

Name _____ Date _____

Time Check!

Time Check	Time Check	Time Check	Time Check
1._____	1._____	1._____	1._____
2._____	2._____	2._____	2._____
3._____	3._____	3._____	3._____
4._____	4._____	4._____	4._____
5._____	5._____	5._____	5._____
6._____	6._____	6._____	6._____
7._____	7._____	7._____	7._____
8._____	8._____	8._____	8._____
9._____	9._____	9._____	9._____
10._____	10._____	10._____	10._____

Name _____

Date _____

TAKE–HOME ACTIVITY

Family Planner

Dear Family,

We are learning about time in school. One concept we are studying is using time to make schedules. Please help your child make a schedule of your family's important activities for the week.

Day: Date:	Day: Date:	Day: Date:	Day: Date:	Day: Date:	Day: Date:	Day: Date:
Activity:	Activity:	Activity:	Activity:	Activity:	Activity:	Activity:
Time:	Time:	Time:	Time:	Time:	Time:	Time:
Activity:	Activity:	Activity:	Activity:	Activity:	Activity:	Activity:
Time:	Time:	Time:	Time:	Time:	Time:	Time:

Best-Ever Activities for Grades 2-3: Time & Money Scholastic Professional Books

42

Name _____   Date _____

Make a Theme Clock

Best-Ever Activities for Grades 2–3: Time & Money   Scholastic Professional Books

43

Name _____ Date _____

Design a Coin

Best-Ever Activities for Grades 2–3: Time & Money Scholastic Professional Books

Name _____   Date _____

Rolling for Coins

Player 1		Player 2	
Number of Coins	Value	Number of Coins	Value

Name _____ Date _____

Pocket Change

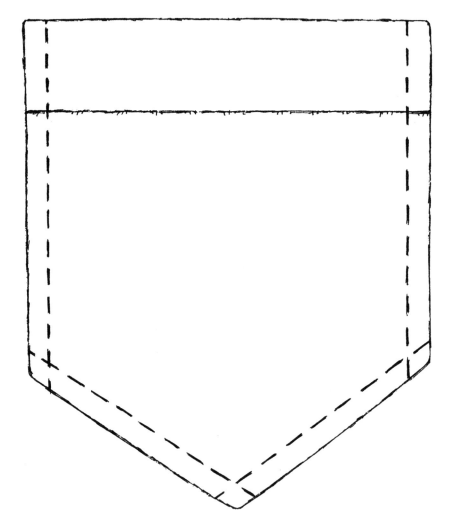

Estimate 1: _____   Estimate 2: _____

Actual Amount: _____

Best-Ever Activities for Grades 2–3: Time & Money   Scholastic Professional Books

Name _____   Date _____

Coin Chart

	Penny	Nickel	Dime	Quarter
Value				
Picture on Head				
Picture on Tail				
Amount in One Dollar				
Color				
Other Details				

Best-Ever Activities for Grades 2–3: Time & Money   Scholastic Professional Books

Name _____   Date _____

Counting and Comparing Coins

Dear Family,
We're learning how to count and compare coins. Use real, plastic, or cutout coins to solve the riddles. Draw the coins to show each answer. Please return this paper to school by_____ .

I have three coins. The total amount is 25 cents.
What coins do I have?

_____

I have five coins. The total amount is 21 cents.
What coins do I have?

_____

I have four coins. The total amount is 85 cents.
What coins do I have?

_____

Write your own coin riddle to share with the class.

_____

_____

Best-Ever Activities for Grades 2–3: Time & Money   Scholastic Professional Books